The Art of Picking

taught by...

Photo By R. Andrew Lepley

Online Video

Video
dv.melbay.com/**20402**
You Tube
www.melbay.com/**20402V**

2 3 4 5 6 7 8 9 0

Visit us on the Web at www.melbay.com — E-mail us at email@melbay.com

contents

Acknowledgements

A special thanks to Curt for proof reading this book.

Corey Christiansen of Mel Bay publications. Corey provided invaluable input.

A special thanks to everyone I have ever taught. Teaching has enabled me to formalize this whole concept.

A very special thank you to the following Doctors:

Dr Leonard Harman
Dr. Howard Klein
Dr. Dave Rudick
Dr Eric Goosenberg
Dr. Robin Goosenberg
Dr Barry Keyes
Dr. Mitchel Smith
Dr. Joe Califano
Dr. Brenda Branson
Dr. R Mutreja

Special Thanks:

Concord Records
Roger Sadwosky
and Sadwosky guitars
Raezor's Edge Cabinets
Acoustic Image Amplifiers
Allesandro Amps
Curt Scheller
Mel Bay Records

A very special thank you to Bill Bay, Doug Witherspoon and Corey Christiansen.

Introduction

When I first began to play jazz guitar, I listened mostly to guitarists. A few years later I was introduced to the music of Charlie Parker, John Coltrane, Art Tatum and Oscar Peterson, as well as many other instrumentalists. I mention those four individuals because they had the most effect on my technique and musical style. After a few attempts to copy or imitate horn and piano lines, I soon realized the alternate picking technique which I was using at the time was not going to cut it; I had to find a better way to move the pick across the strings.

I discovered when two notes were not on the same string, the pick had to travel past the string the second note was on and then reverse direction to come back up and play the note. That is a long way for the pick to travel. I found one concept or rule that causes the pick to travel the least amount of distance. The fundamental concept is:

> ▶ **When going to a higher string, use a down-stroke.**
> ▶ **When going to a lower string, use an up-stroke.**
> ▶ **When playing on one string, use alternate strokes**.

This technique creates a significant change in right hand technique, or, I prefer the term "habit." Most guitarists have been using the alternate picking "habit" for many years: that habit is not easy to break. However, with a fair amount of practice and discipline you can break the habit and develop a much more efficient right hand technique.

The Right Hand

The right hand, wrist and elbow should always be relaxed and never tense or tight. The wrist should not move or tilt. The movement should come from the elbow. Do not touch the strings, bridge or any other part of the guitar with the fingers of your right hand. Your palm may rest lightly on the strings.

The Strokes

This technique creates the following strokes:

> ▶ **Down-up:** Everyone can do this one.
> ▶ **Up-down:** A bit more difficult, especially keeping the accent strong. The goal is to make the up-stroke sound as strong and round as the downstroke.
> ▶ **In-between stroke:** This stroke requires the pick to move between two adjacent strings or non-adjacent strings. This stroke is the most difficult to master.
> ▶ **Consecutive down-stroke and consecutive up-stroke:** When practicing this technique it is important to play the notes evenly and with an equal amount of attack. The tendency is to rush the notes that follow the initial stroke. An example would be two, three or four notes, each on an adjacent string, played with a single down or up stroke depending on the direction of the phrase. The consecutive up-stroke is harder to control.

I have attempted to cover most situations that a guitarist might encounter, but it is impossible to cover them all. Music and guitar have an infinite number of possibilities.

Symbols

‒

⊓ = Down-stroke

∨ = Up-stroke

Some of the exercises require you to start the exercise with both a down stroke then an up stroke. See exercise 23 on page 25.

If you follow the uppermost picking indicators, you will see that the Ist eighth note has an up stroke, the next eighth note has a down stroke and the 3rd eighth note has an up stroke. It doesn't matter which way you start, by the 3rd or 4th stroke, you will be at the same stroke whether you started with an up or a down. You can see that by the 3rd stroke (an up stroke) you are in sync with the lower indicators where you started with a down stroke. Since there are only two strokes, this should be obvious. I recommend that you practice all the exercises starting with both strokes. There should be only a very slight difference in sound.

If you have been playing a long time, you will find it very difficult to change your picking technique or "habit". But all habits can be broken. It will take a little patience and a moderate amount of practice. At first, your technique will suffer. This is only natural since you are incorporating something that is foreign to your brain and hands. When this new picking technique becomes a habit, your speed and accuracy will improve. How long this will take, will vary with how much time you practice. I recommend you practice these exercise at MM 60 to 120 then increase your speed from there.

It is impossible to cover all the possible picking scenarios. Music has an infinite number of possibilities. I have attempted to describe the techniques that I use when improvising various phrases. The exercises are designed to take the student from point A to Z. It is not a good idea to skip around in this book.

Hope you enjoy this book,

Sincerely,

Jimmy Bruno

The Strokes

▼

The down-up stroke

This is the most common stroke on the guitar. Use this exercise to control your accent on the downbeats. Apply to all strings.

exercise 1

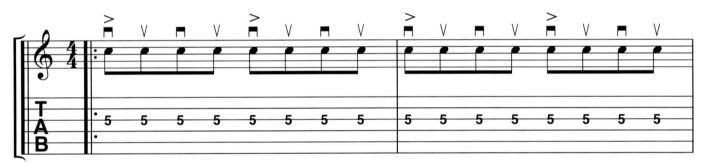

Practice keeping your wrist straight but not stiff. Remember: the movement is from the elbow.

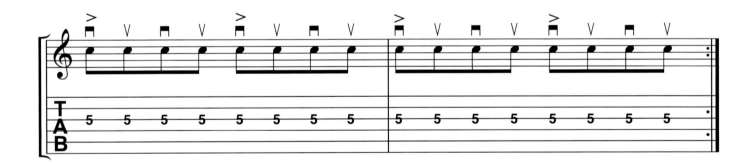

The up-down stroke

Use this exercise to control your accent on the downbeats but with an up-stroke. Apply to all strings.

exercise 2

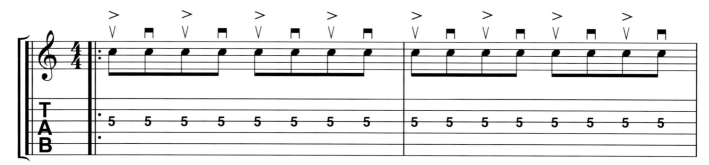

Do not touch the guitar with the fingers of the right hand.

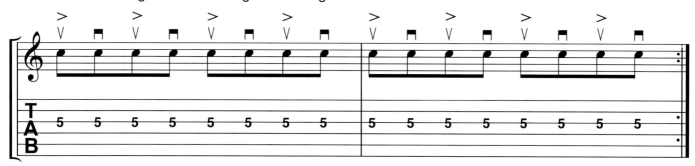

Mixed strokes

This exercise is designed to alternate the accents with a down-stroke then an up-stroke. Apply to all strings.

exercise 3

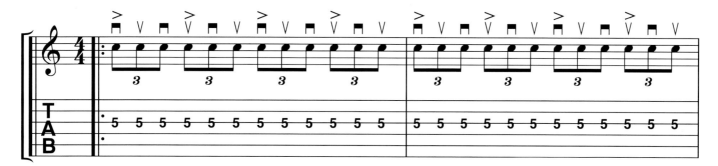

Do not touch the pick guard or strings with the fingers of the right hand.

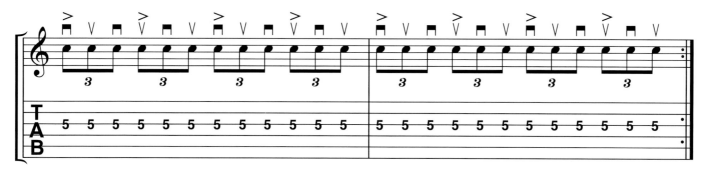

In between stroke

This is the hardest stroke to master. It involves going between two adjacent strings. This is a critical part of your right hand technique. Take your time with this one. Apply to any two adjacent strings using the double-stop of your choice. Do not let notes ring!

exercise 4

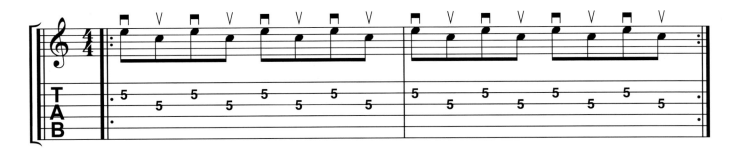

exercise 5

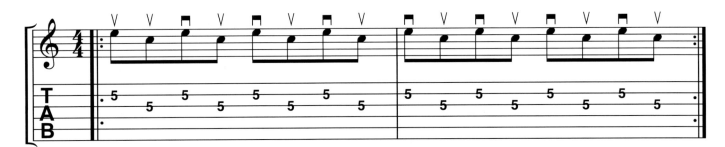

Consecutive Strokes

Consecutive "Down" to "up" strokes

This exercise gets more into the real world as this type thing occurs in many jazz phrases.
Apply to any two adjacent strings using the double stop of your choice. **Do not let notes ring!**

exercise 6

Consecutive "Up " to "Down " strokes

Same as previous exercise but in reverse. **Do not let notes ring!**

exercise 7

It is necessary to play the previous two exercises evenly. At this stage, precision of the 8th notes is more important than speed.

Triplets

The following exercise uses a major triad with a triplet rhythm. Although it is possible, I have found when playing triplets with a repeating pattern such as a triad or some other pattern, it is better to break the rule. Instead of playing the exercise like this,

exercise 8

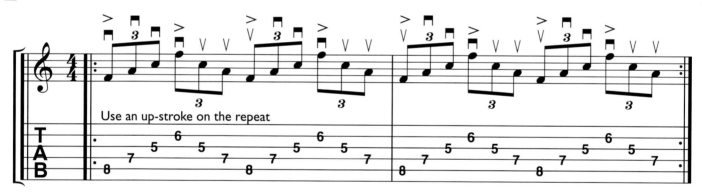

Use an up-stroke on the repeat

use three "down-strokes" followed by three "up-strokes". Apply to any three note chord on any three adjacent strings. This exercise is designed to practice three consecutive strokes in the same direction.

exercise 8
continued

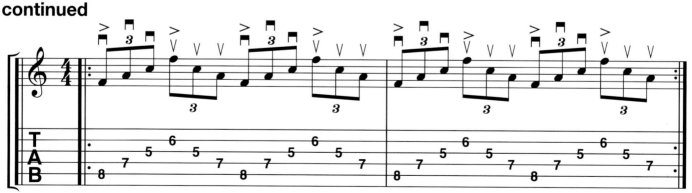

However, if I had to play a triplet phrase in the context of a line and not in an exercise, I would adhere to the rule. The following phrase illustrates my point.

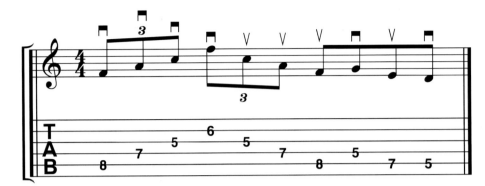

The next exercise illustrates triplets with the rule applied. This is more likely to occur in a jazz phrase.

exercise 9

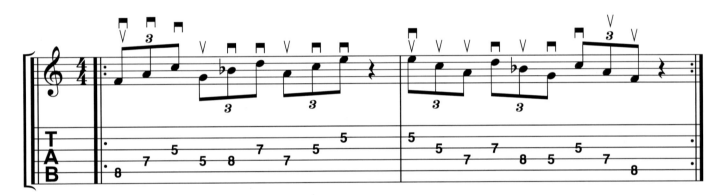

or like this with 16th notes. Pay close attention to the accents.

Sixteenth notes

This exercise requires you to reverse direction on the same string. A common stroke {bat happens with repeated notes. Apply this exercise to any four note chord anywhere on the guitar.

exercise 10

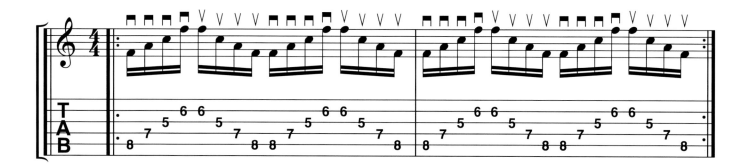

exercise 11

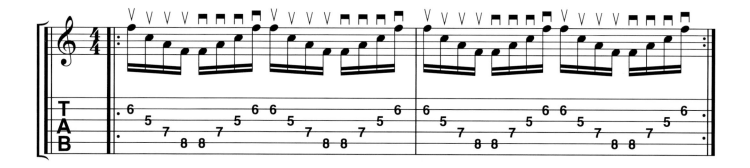

The Major Scales

Picking applied to Major scale fingering 6V2

Below are the six basic fingerings for the major scales. This will give you an idea how the rule works on any scale or scale type passage For more info on these fingerings see my book "Six Essential Fingerings for the Jazz Guitarist" at www.jimmybruno.com.

exercise 12

▲ = moving to HIGHER STRING
▼ = moving to LOWER STRING

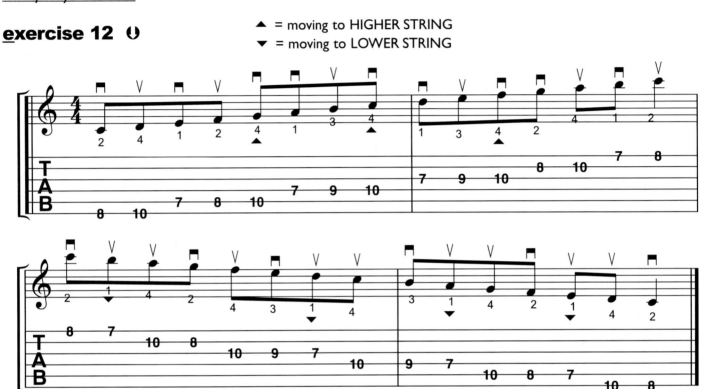

Picking applied to Major scale fingering 5V2

exercise 13

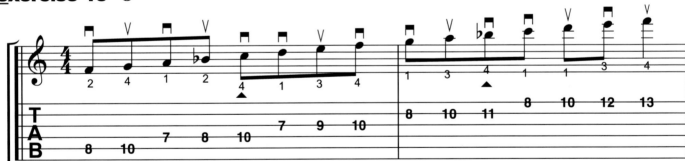

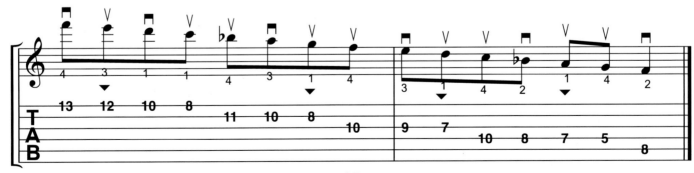

Picking applied to Major scale fingering 6V4

exercise 14

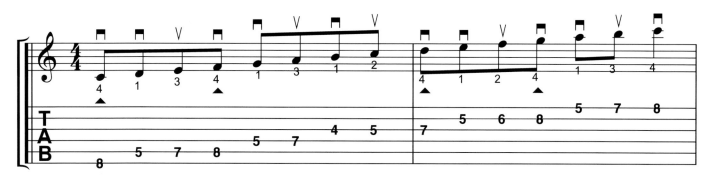

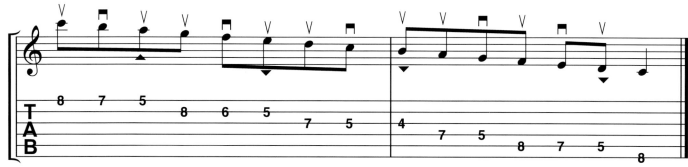

Picking applied to Major scale fingering 5V4

exercise 15

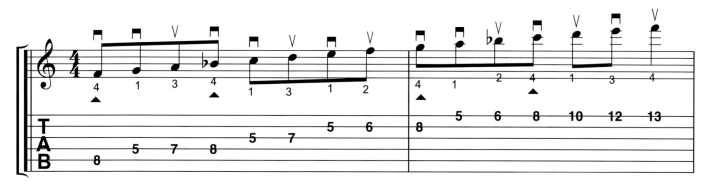

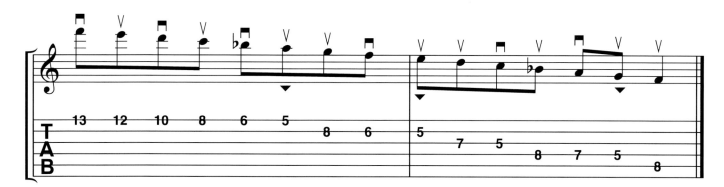

Picking applied to Major scale fingering 6H2

exercise 16 ↺

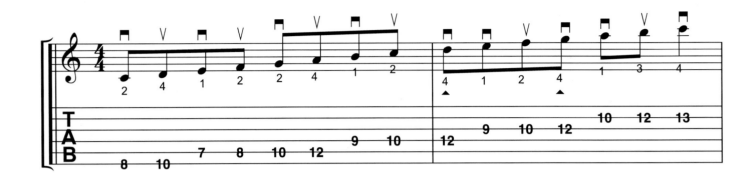

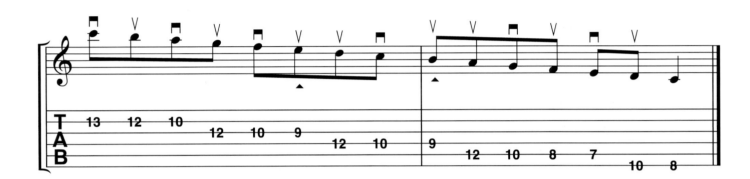

Picking applied to Major scale fingering 5H2

exercise 17 ↺   * Between exercises 17 & 18 there is bonus footage of Jimmy playing scales through the circle of 4ths.

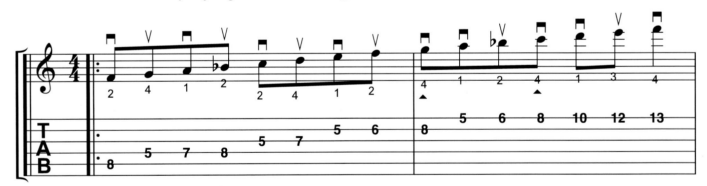

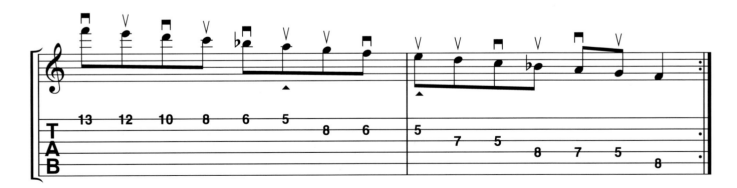

Arpeggios

Although this is not a book about arpeggios, I feel it is important to include a few basic arpeggios so that you can see the picking method applied to arpeggios. The difficulty with any arpeggio exercise, is keeping the notes from ringing. Articulation is more important hand speed.

Major 7ths vertical

exercise 18

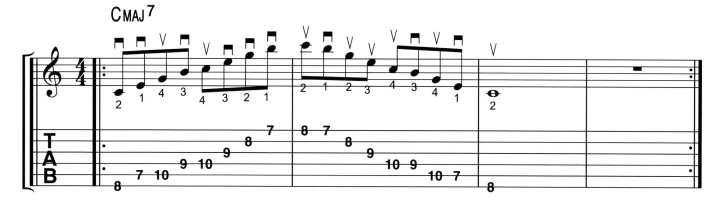

exercise 19

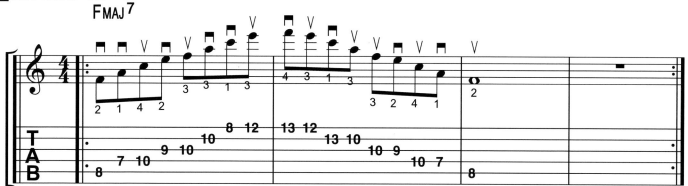

Major 7ths horizontal

exercise 20

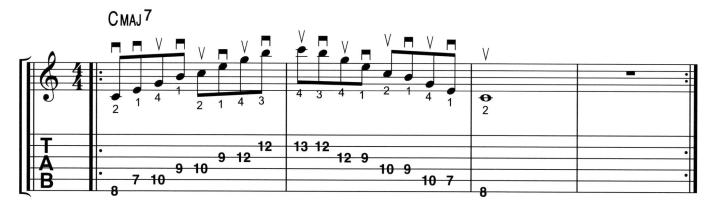

Major 7ths <u>horizontal</u>

exercise 21

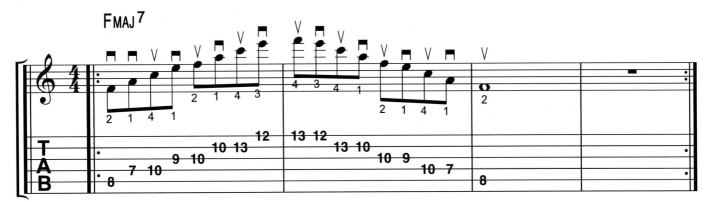

Minor 7ths <u>vertical</u>

exercise 22

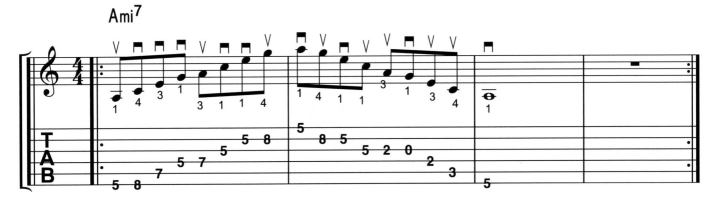

exercise 23

Minor 7ths horizontal

exercise 24

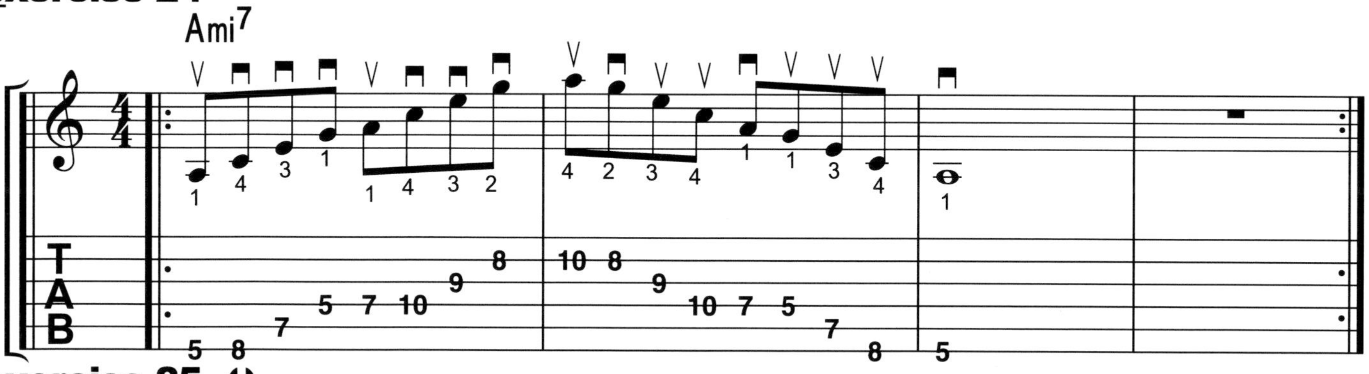

exercise 25

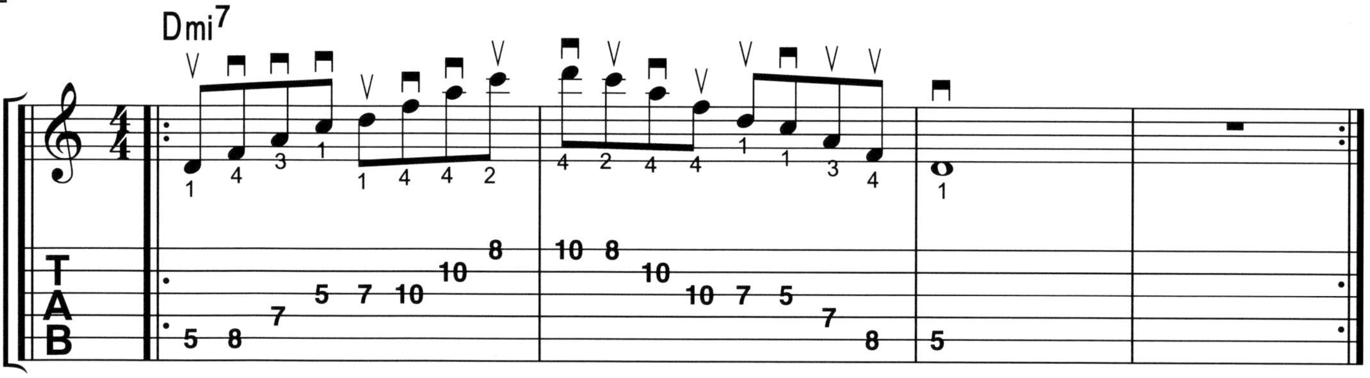

Major triad exercises:

This makes a great warm-up exercise. It is very difficult to play with clean articulation. The result is well worth the time. This exercise alone will facilitate the separation of notes with any phrase that contains an arpeggio or arpeggio fragment.

exercise 26

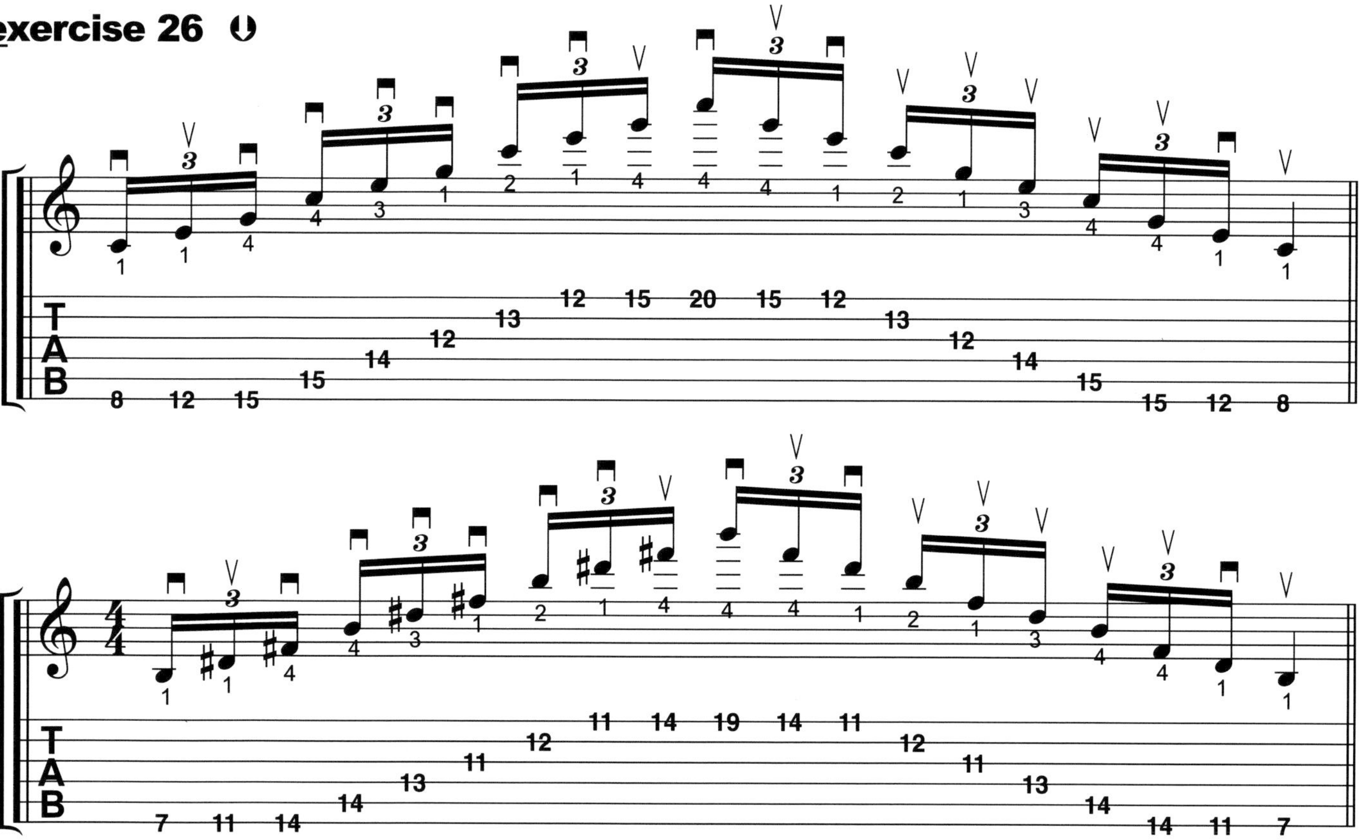

Fingering and picking is the same throughout.

exercise 26 ↻
cont.

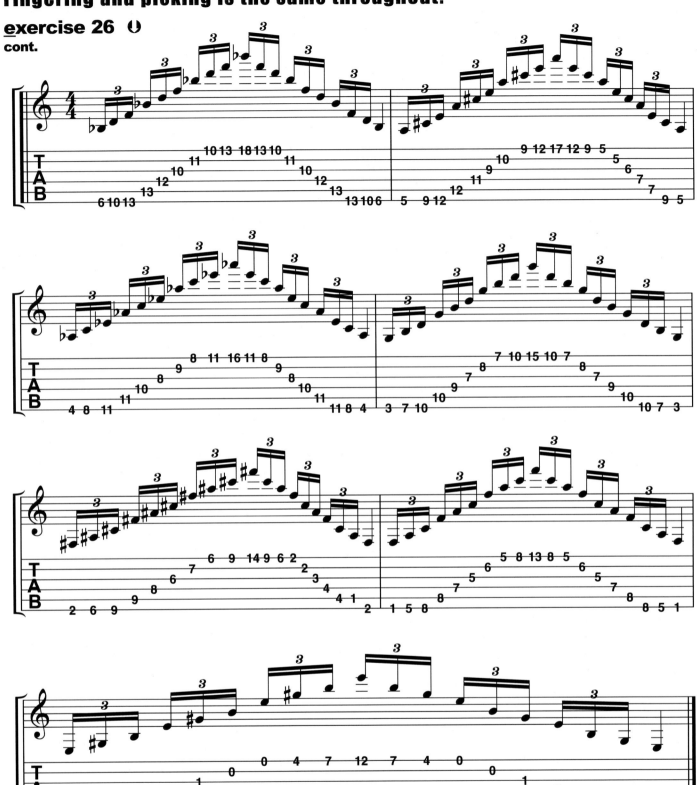

Minor 9 arpeggios:

I have seen this referred to as sweep picking. I see no reason to make any distinction. Everything follows the rule:

exercise 27   Higher string = "down stroke"   Lower string = "up stroke"

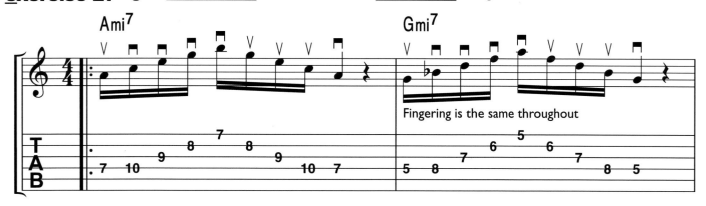

Fingering is the same throughout

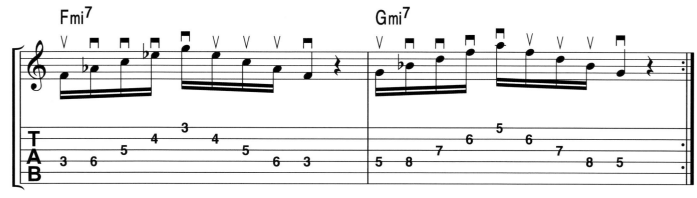

Minor 11 arpeggios:

Because of the fingering it is possible to play 6 notes in one beat (sextuplet.) The fingering sets up the consecutive down and up strokes to go across four strings. Saxophone players and pianists use phrases like this.

exercise 28

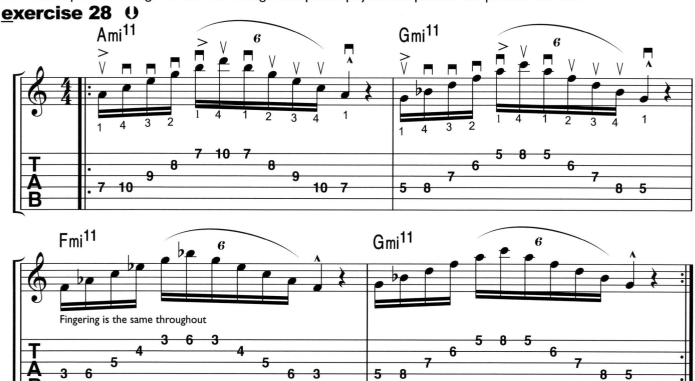

Fingering is the same throughout

Minor 11 arpeggios:

This is more of the same but with groups of quintuplets.

exercise 29

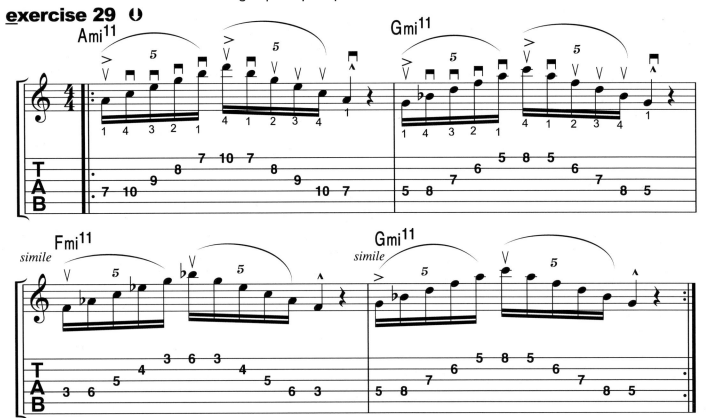

Minor 9th arpeggios:

Below are several ways to pick this. Again, the fingering makes the speed possible.

exercise 30

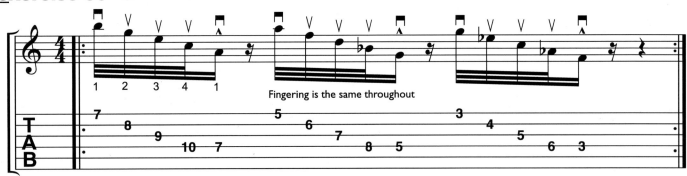

I have found when there is a rest between phrases, it is possible to break the rule and use whatever stroke you please to start the phrase. Below I used an up stroke to start each phrase.

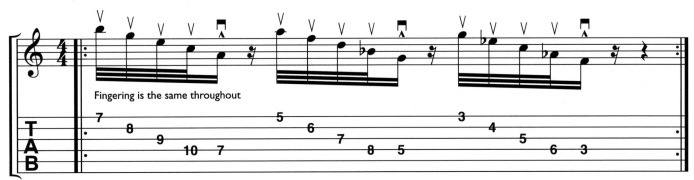

Try starting any phrase with both strokes, down and up. There should be only a slight difference in sound.

Minor 9th arpeggios:

By using fingerings that place notes on adjacent strings, either higher or lower, these large two octave arpeggios become possible.

exercise 31

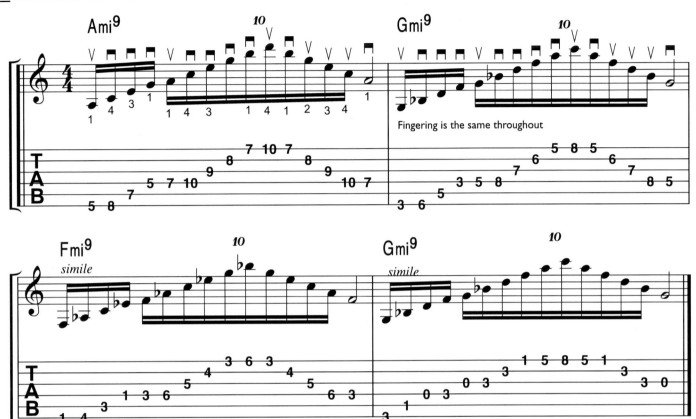

To illustrate all the possible arpeggios is beyond the scope of this book. The main point to remember is that the fingering will determine the picking. By placing as many notes of an arpeggio on adjacent strings, the easier the so called "sweep" becomes. I am not fond of that term; to me there is only one way to think about it: "When going to a **higher string** always use a **"down stroke"**; when going to a **lower string** always use an **"up stroke."** I often run across guitarists who become misled into thinking that picking for single lines is different than picking for arpeggios. You have to be careful to NOT let the **fingerboard** make the music. The music comes from inside; the picking mechanism described in this book is designed to make it easier for the music to be realized.

String Skipping

Skipping Strings

When skipping strings the same rule applies: when going to a higher string use a down-stroke; when going to a lower string, use an up-stroke.

exercise 32 ↻

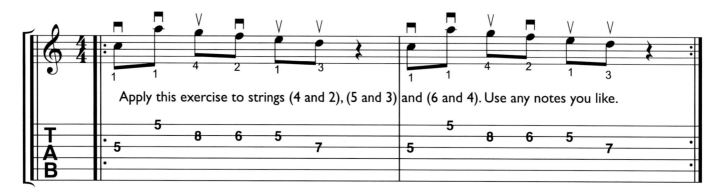

Apply this exercise to strings (4 and 2), (5 and 3) and (6 and 4). Use any notes you like.

Here's the same thing in the opposite direction.

exercise 33 ↻

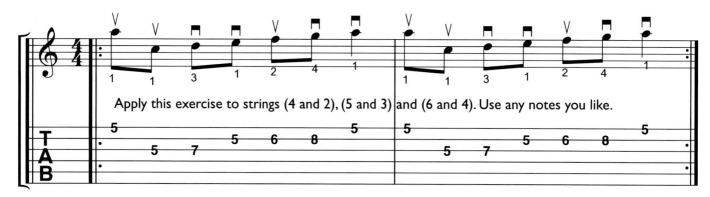

Apply this exercise to strings (4 and 2), (5 and 3) and (6 and 4). Use any notes you like.

This exercise is a bit more difficult. It uses the same exercise but with the "In-between -stroke".

exercise 34 ↻

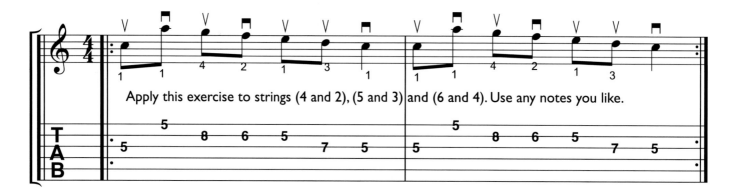

Apply this exercise to strings (4 and 2), (5 and 3) and (6 and 4). Use any notes you like.

Here's the same thing in the opposite direction.

exercise 35

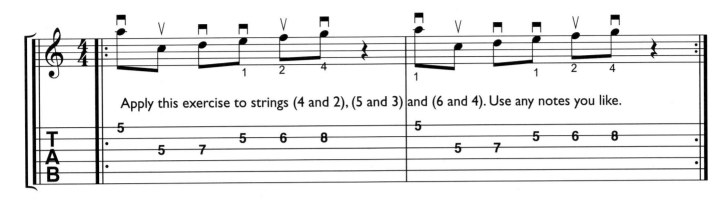

Consecutive down-up strokes with a string skip.

START THIS EXERCISE WITH BOTH STROKES, DOWN AND UP

exercise 36

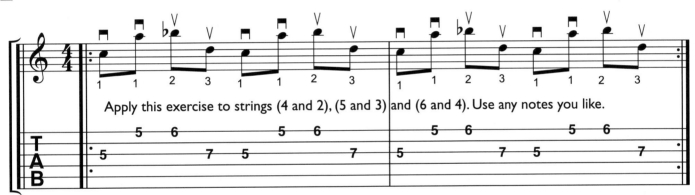

Consecutive up-down strokes with a string skip.

START THIS EXERCISE WITH BOTH STROKES, DOWN AND UP

exercise 37

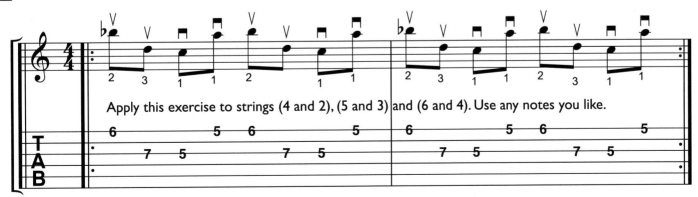

Sixth with a string skip.

START THIS EXERCISE WITH BOTH STROKES, DOWN AND UP

exercise 38

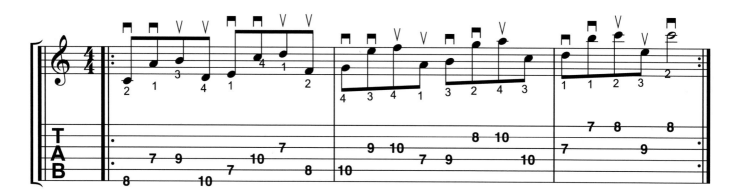

START THIS EXERCISE WITH BOTH STROKES, DOWN AND UP

exercise 39

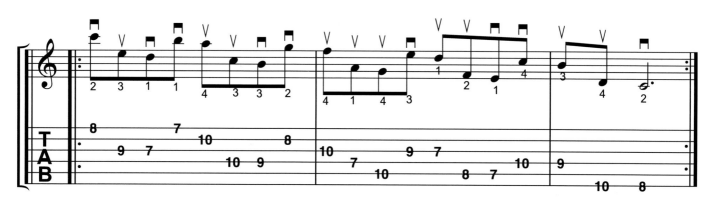

In-Between stroke with a string skip.

START THIS EXERCISE WITH BOTH STROKES, DOWN AND UP

exercise 40

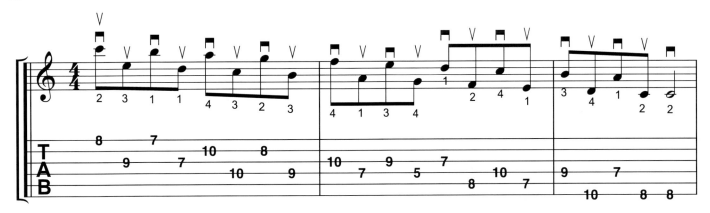

This exercise is very difficult to master. You need to put an accent on the "up-stroke" while skipping a string. It uses the "in-between" stroke with a string skip. You should also practice this with an alternate stroke. I find that when playing exercises like this it is easier to play them with alternating "down" - "up" strokes.

START THIS EXERCISE WITH BOTH STROKES, DOWN AND UP

exercise 41

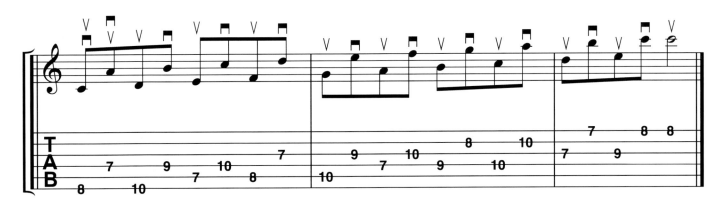

Be-Bop Phrases

exercise 42

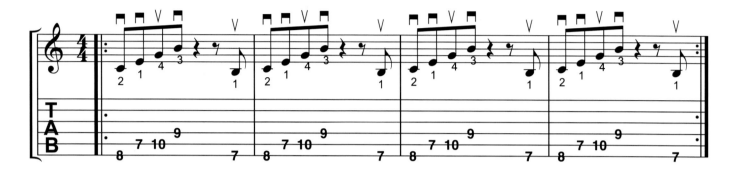

exercise 43

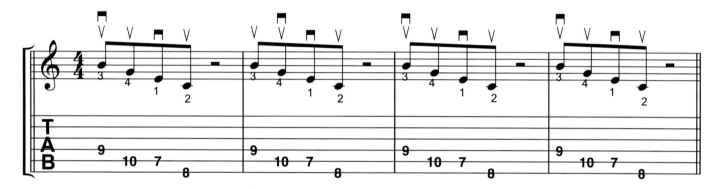

exercise 44

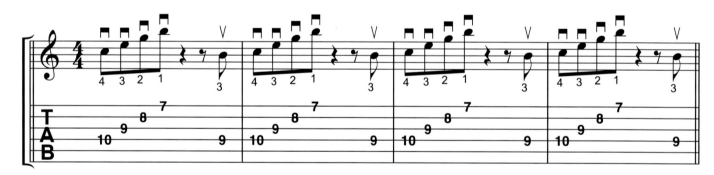

exercise 45

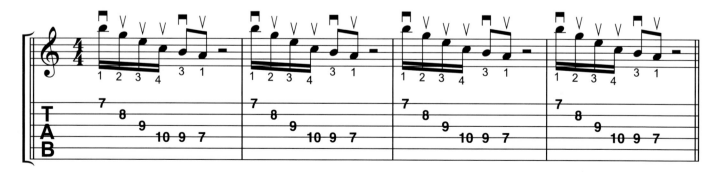

exercise 46

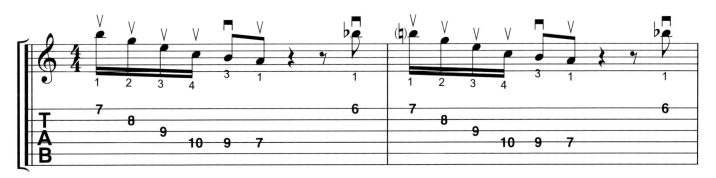

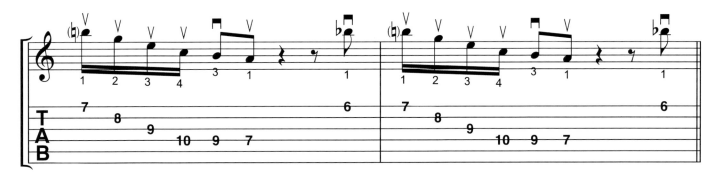

exercise 47

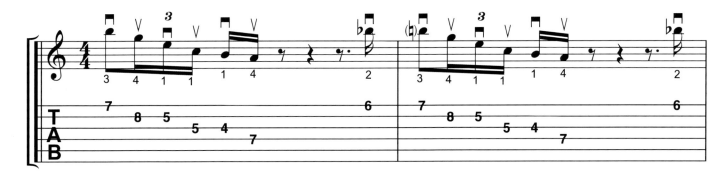

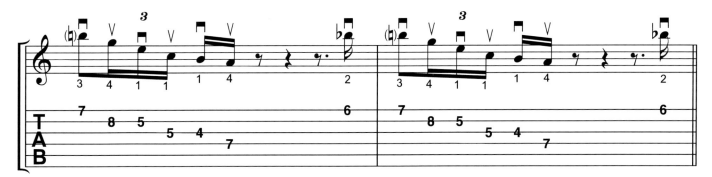

exercise 48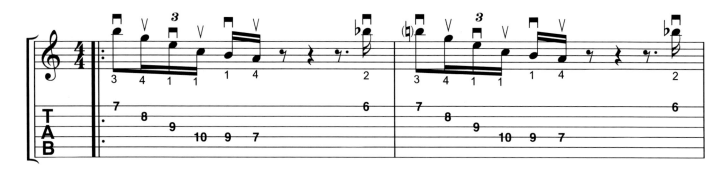

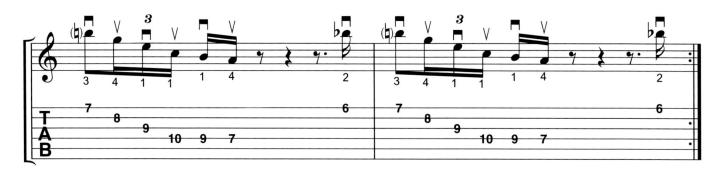

exercise 49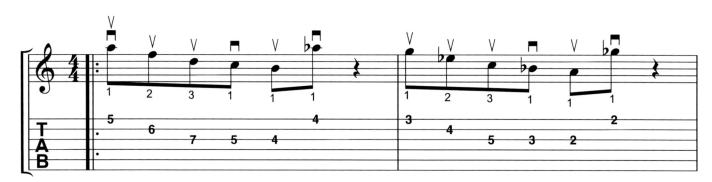

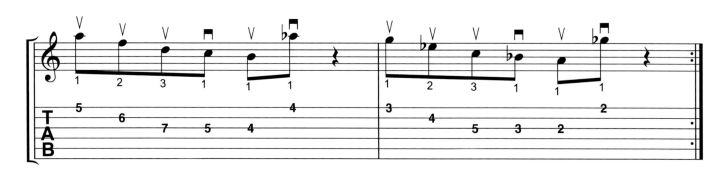

Here's the same phrase in the 7th position. This changes the picking considerably.

exercise 50   (7th position)

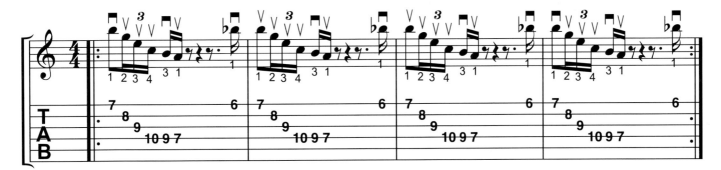

exercise 51

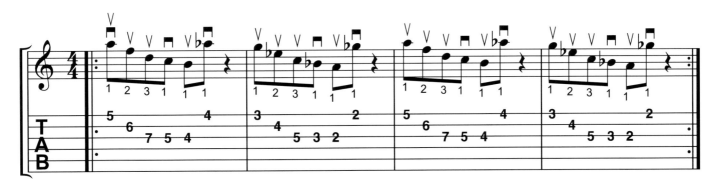

exercise 52

exercise 53

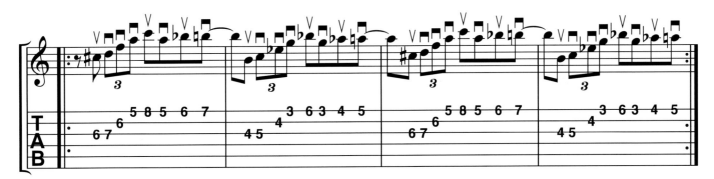

Slurred Triplets

exercise 54

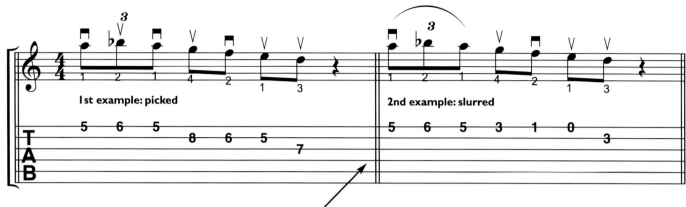

I prefer the **2nd example**; it sounds more horn-like.

Learn how to slur triplets with a "down-stroke" and an "up-stroke."

exercise 55    ### exercise 56

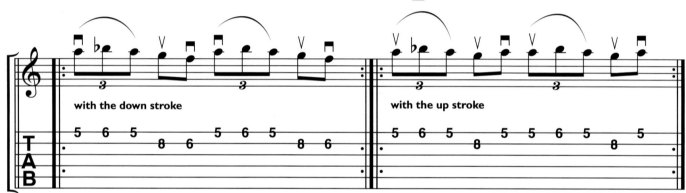

exercise 57

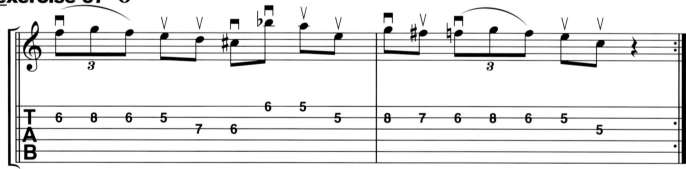

Same example starting with an "up-sroke".

exercise 58

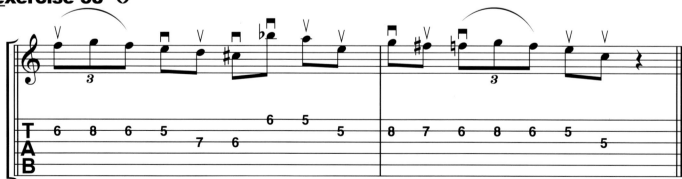

Articulations

I think of articulations as inflections. When someone is speaking not all the words have the same accent, volume, inflection etc. When playing lines you need to alter the inflection of the notes; not all the notes are long or short or accented. These inflections are accomplished by slurring notes. Pick one note and play two notes. The following exercises illustrate this point. They are all typical be-bop phrases.

exercise 59

The same phrase in a different position:

exercise 60

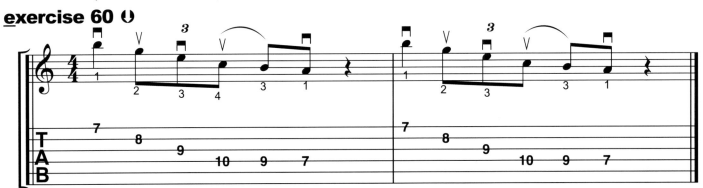

Here's a typical be-bop phrase. Notice how the different articulations affect the sound.

Here is the phrase without slurs:

exercise 61

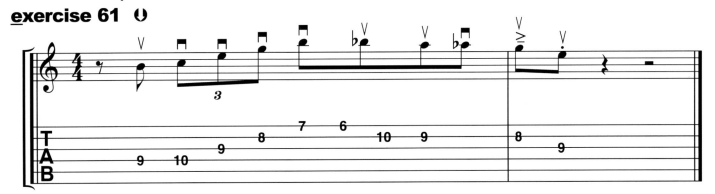

Here is the phrase with one slur:

exercise 62 ○

Make sure you play these last two notes, long, short.

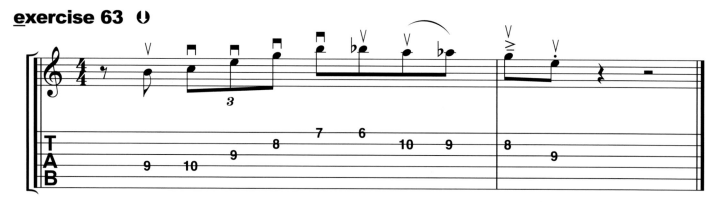

Here is the phrase with the slur moved to the next beat.

exercise 63 ○

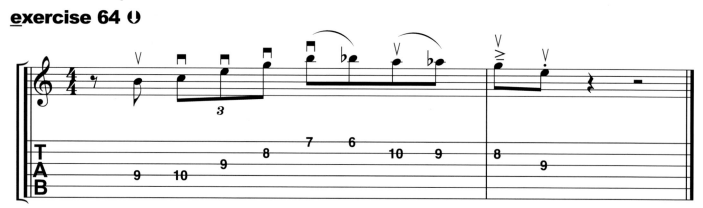

Here is the phrase with two slurs

exercise 64 ○

No slurs:
exercise 65

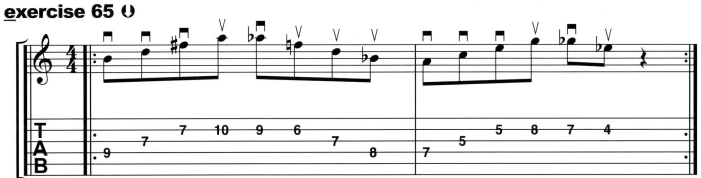

Try moving the slur over any two notes that are on the same string.

With slurs:
exercise 66

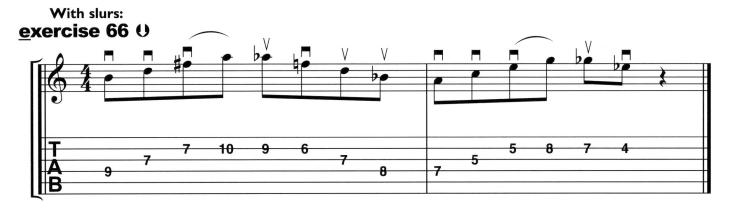

I've added a few slurs. Experiment adding your own slurs in different places.

exercise 67

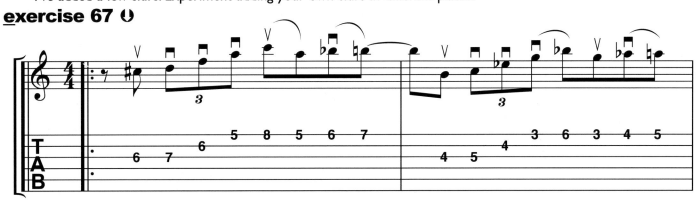

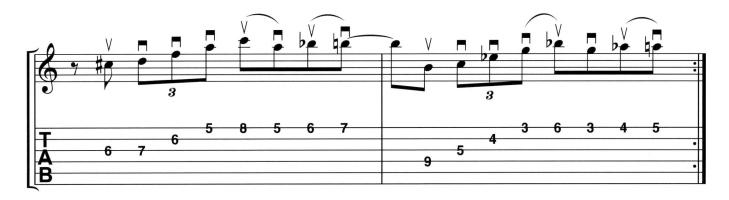

Breaking the Rules

There are special circumstances where it may be desirable to break the rules. In the example below, I use consecutive down strokes to emphasize certain notes. This type picking is useful when you are trying to emulate a big band type phrase.

exercise 68

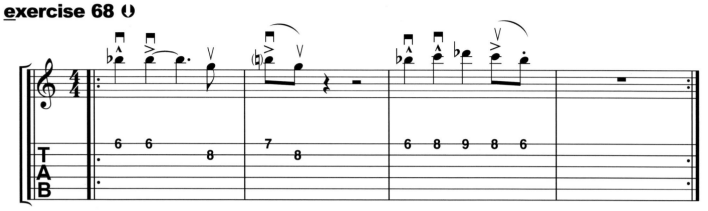

Here is the same type phrase with slurs.

exercise 69

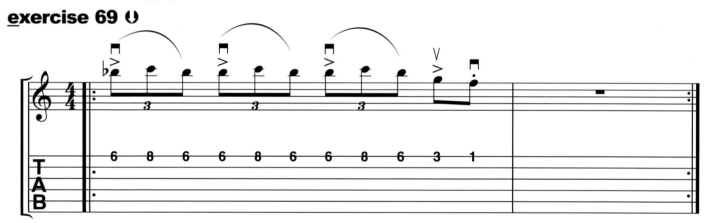

When there is a rhythmic break between notes you may want to use down strokes.

exercise 70

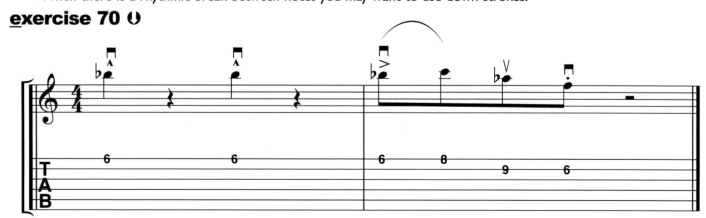

Conclusion

Picking is a habit. Habits are hard to break but not impossible. The longer you have been playing, the harder it will be to change. With a moderate amount of practice and a lot of patience, anyone can improve their technique. The key is repetition. Do not overanalyze your right hand movements. After a short time, these strokes will become second nature. If you have any questions or comments, feel free to email me at jimmy@jimmybruno.com.

About The Author

One would be hard pressed to find another jazz guitarist so polished, sought-after and committed to the music that he loves. From his earliest days, Jimmy Bruno has loved and been loved by jazz. With his unmistakable presence and inspiring virtuosity, he has become a legend in his own time.

Born in Philadelphia on July 22, 1953, Jimmy Bruno was first exposed to music by his parents at a very early age. His mother was a singer and his father, Jimmy Bruno, Sr., was a notable jazz guitarist who was best known for his performance in 1959 on the hit recording "Guitar Boogie Shuffle" with Frank Virtue and the Virtues. When Bruno was about eight his childhood love for music began to develop when his father brought home what would be Jimmy's first guitar. As a child, he never had any formal training, but instead absorbed the life altering sounds of Johnny Smith, Hank Garland, Ella Fitzgerald, Charlie Parker, Art Tatum, John Coltrane and Oscar Peterson.

In 1973, when Bruno was just nineteen, he landed his first big gig when Buddy Rich came to Philly holding auditions for a guitarist. He spent the next year on the road with Buddy, receiving quite a musical education. When he returned to Philadelphia in 1974, he found few gigs as a jazz musician and decided to try his luck playing in Las Vegas, finally settling in Los Angeles as a studio musician. In the end it wasn't the place or the music he loved. Since his return to Philly in 1988, Jimmy Bruno has created a name that is synonymous with jazz guitar, recording numerous albums for Concord Records and now for Mel Bay Records.

In addition to his new album with Mel Bay Records, Jimmy Bruno has recently been featured in three, live concert DVDs released through Mel Bay Records - *Jimmy Bruno: Live at Chris' Café, Volumes 1 and 2 and Jimmy Bruno and Jack Wilkins: Live at The Theatre.* Jimmy is also a Mel Bay author who to date has written several instructional books for six and seven string jazz guitar. Jimmy Bruno is co-chair of the Jazz Guitar Department at the University of the Arts in Philadelphia, PA and is a featured writer for *Just Jazz Guitar Magazine.*

Visit www.jimmybruno.com or for help with this book please email me at jimmy@jimmybruno.com

Other Products by Jimmy Bruno

Product Number	Title	Format
MB99148DVD	Jimmy Bruno & Jack Wilkins: Live from the Theatre at Washington, Virginia	DVD
MB99147DVD	Cafe Benedetto	DVD
MB20523DVD	Jimmy Bruno Live at Chris' Jazz Cafe Jimmy	DVD
MB20559DVD	Bruno Live at Chris' Jazz Cafe Vol. 2 Six	DVD
MB20001	Essential Fingerings for the Jazz Guitarist	Book

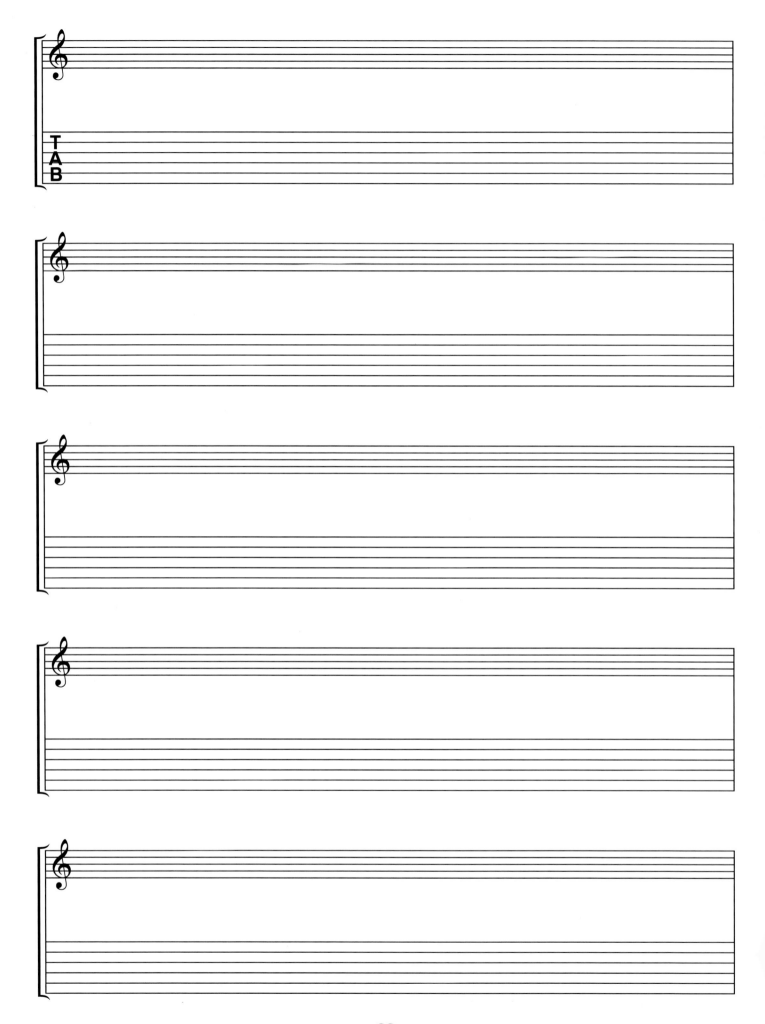

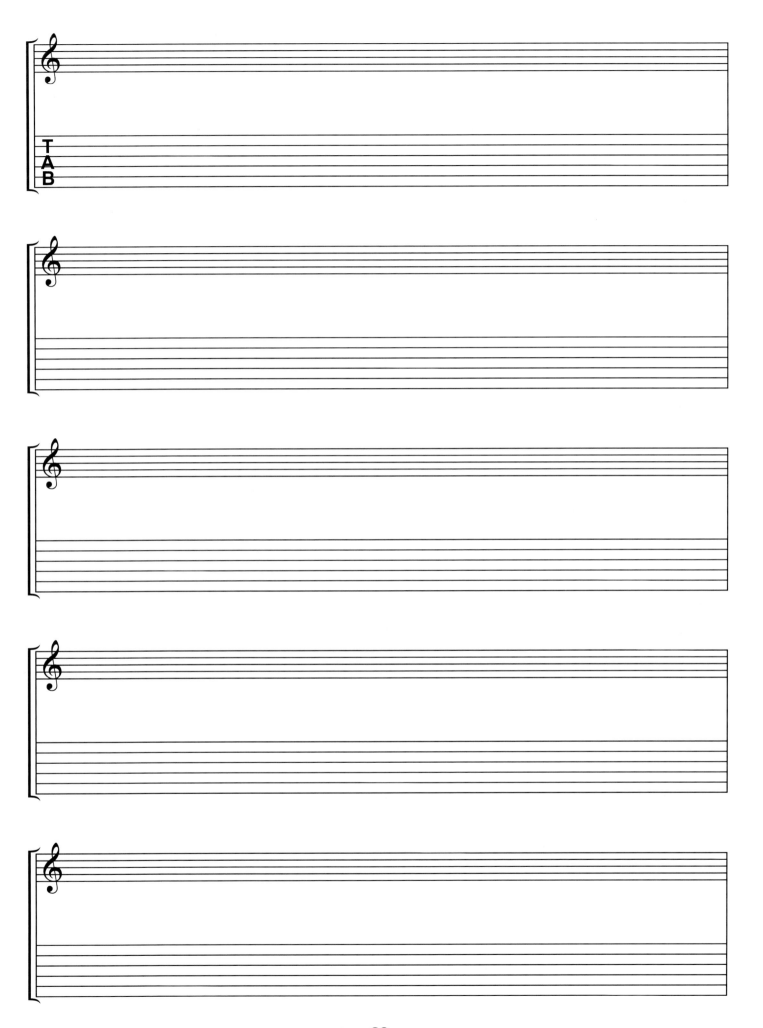